C000008455

Jesus

TRUTHFUL REVEALER

BILL DONAHUE
& KERI WYATT KENT

IVP Connect

InterVarsity Press
Downers Grove, Illinois

Inter-Varsity Press
Leicester, England

InterVarsity Press, USA
P.O. Box 1400, Downers Grove, IL 60515-1426, USA
World Wide Web: www.ivpress.com
E-mail: mail@ivpress.com

Inter-Varsity Press, England
38 De Montfort Street, Leicester LE1 7GP, England
Website: www.ivpbooks.com
E-mail: ivp@ivp-editorial.co.uk

InterVarsity Press®, USA, is the book-publishing division of InterVarsity Christian Fellowship/USA®, a student movement active on campus at hundreds of universities, colleges and schools of nursing in the United States of America, and a member movement of the International Fellowship of Evangelical Students. For information about local and regional activities, write Public Relations Dept., InterVarsity Christian Fellowship/USA, 6400 Schroeder Rd., P.O. Box 7895, Madison, WI 53707-7895, or visit the IVCF website at <www.intervarsity.org>.

Inter-Varsity Press, England, is the publishing division of the Universities and Colleges Christian Fellowship (formerly the Inter-Varsity Fellowship), a student movement linking Christian Unions in universities and colleges throughout Great Britain, and a member movement of the International Fellowship of Evangelical Students. For information about local and national activities write to UCCF, 38 De Montfort Street, Leicester LE1 7GP, email us at email@uccf.org.uk, or visit the UCCF website at www.uccf.org.uk.

All Scripture quotations, unless otherwise indicated, are taken from the Holy Bible, New International Version®. NIV®. Copyright © 1973, 1978, 1984 by International Bible Society. Used by permission of Zondervan Publishing House. Distributed in the U.K. by permission of Hodder and Stoughton Ltd. All rights reserved. "NIV" is a registered trademark of International Bible Society. UK trademark number 1448790.

Design: Cindy Kiple
Images: Burke/Triolo Productions/Getty Images

USA ISBNs   0-8308-2153-8
            978-0-8308-2153-2

UK ISBNs   1-84474-119-2
            978-1-84474-119-9

Printed in the United States of America ∞

P	19	18	17	16	15	14	13	12	11	10	9	8	7	6	5	4	3	2	1
Y	19	18	17	16	15	14	13	12	11	10	09	08	07	06	05					

CONTENTS

BEFORE YOU BEGIN

The Jesus 101 series is designed to help you respond to Jesus as you encounter him in the stories and teachings of the Bible, particularly the Gospel accounts of the New Testament. The "101" designation does not mean "simple"; it means "initial." You probably took introductory-level courses in high school or at a university, like Economics 101 or Biology 101. Each was an initial course, a first encounter with the teachings and principles of the subject matter. I had my first encounter with economic theory in Econ 101, but it was not necessarily simple or always easy (at least not for me!).

Jesus 101 may be the first time you looked closely at Jesus. For the first time you will encounter his grace and love, be exposed to his passion and mission, and get a firsthand look at the way he connects with people like you and me. Or perhaps, like me, you have been a Christian many years. In that case you will encounter Jesus for the first time all over again. Often when I read a biblical account of an event in Jesus' life, even if the text is very familiar to me, I am amazed at a new insight or a fresh, personal connection with Jesus I hadn't experienced before.

I believe Jesus 101 will challenge your thinking and stir your soul regardless of how far along the spiritual pathway you might be. After all, Jesus is anything but dull: he tended to shake up the world of everyone who interacted with him. Sometimes people sought him out; often he surprised them. In every case, he challenged them, evoking a reaction they could hardly ignore.

There are many ways we might encounter Jesus. In this series we will focus on eight. You will come face to face with Jesus as

- Provocative Teacher
- Sacred Friend
- Extreme Forgiver
- Authentic Leader
- Truthful Revealer
- Compassionate Healer
- Relentless Lover
- Supreme Conqueror

☐ HOW THESE GUIDES ARE PUT TOGETHER

In each of the discussion guides you will find material for six group meetings, though feel free to use as many meetings as necessary to cover the material. That is up to you. Each group will find its way. The important thing is to encounter and connect with Christ, listen to what he is saying, watch what he is doing—and then personalize that encounter individually and as a group.

The material is designed to help you engage with one another, with the Bible and with the person of Jesus. The experiences below are designed to guide you along when you come together as a group.

Gathering to Listen

This short section orients you to the material by using an illustration, a quote or a text that raises probing questions, makes provocative assumptions or statements, or evokes interpersonal tension or thoughtfulness. It may just make you laugh. It sets the tone for the dialogue you will be having together. Take a moment here to connect with one another and focus your attention on the reading. Listen carefully as thoughts and emotions are stirred.

After the reading, you will have an opportunity to respond in some way. What are your first impressions, your assumptions, disagreements, feelings? What comes to mind as you read this?

Encountering Jesus

Here you meet Jesus as he is described in the Bible text. You will encounter his teachings, his personal style and his encounters with people much like you. This section will invite your observations, questions and initial reactions to what Jesus is saying and doing.

Joining the Conversation

A series of group questions and interactions will encourage your little community to engage with one another about the person and story of Jesus. Here you will remain for a few moments in the company of Jesus and of one another. This section may pose a question about your group or ask you to engage in an exercise or interaction with one another. The goal is to discover a sense of community as you question and discover what God is doing.

Connecting Our Stories

Here you are invited to connect your story (life, issues, questions, challenges) with Jesus' story (his teaching, character and actions). We look at our background and history, the things that encourage or disappoint us. We seek to discover what God is doing in our life and the lives of others, and we develop a sense of belonging and understanding.

Finding Our Way

A final section of comments and questions invites you to investigate next steps for your spiritual journey as a group and personally. It will evoke and prompt further action, decisions or conversations in response to what was discovered and discussed. You will prompt one another to listen to God more deeply, take relational risks and invite God's work in your group and in the community around you.

Praying Together

God's Holy Spirit is eager to teach you! Remember that learning is not just a mental activity; it involves relationship and action. One educator suggests that all learning is the result of failed expectations. We hope, then, that at some point your own expectations will fail, that you will be ambushed by the truth and stumble into new and unfamiliar territory that startles you into new ways of thinking about God and relating to him through Christ. And so prayer—talking and listening to God—is a vital part of the Jesus 101 journey.

If you are seeking to discover Jesus for the first time, your prayer can be a very simple expression of your thoughts and questions to God. It may include emotions like anger, frustration, joy or wonder. If you already have an intimate, conversational relationship with God, your prayer will reflect the deepest longings and desires of your soul. Prayer is an integral part of the spiritual life, and small groups are a great place to explore it.

☐ How Do I Prepare?

No preparation is required! Reading the Bible text ahead of time, if you can, will provide an overview of what lies ahead and will give you an opportunity to reflect on the Bible passages. But you will not feel out of the loop or penalized in some way if you do not get to it. This material is designed for *group* discovery and interaction. A sense of team and community develops and excitement grows as you explore the material together. In contrast to merely discussing what everyone has already discovered prior to the meeting, "discovery in the moment" evokes a sense of shared adventure.

If you want homework, do that after each session. Decide how you might face your week, your job, your relationships and family in light of what you have just discovered about Jesus.

☐ A FINAL NOTE

These studies are based on the book *In the Company of Jesus.* It is not required that you read the book to do any Jesus 101 study—each stands alone. But you might consider reading the parallel sections of the book to enrich your experience between small group meetings. The major sections of the book take up the same eight ways that we encounter Jesus in the Jesus 101 guides. So the eight guides mirror the book in structure and themes, but the material in the book is not identical to that of the guides.

Jesus 101 probes more deeply into the subject matter, whereas *In the Company of Jesus* is designed for devotional and contemplative reading and prayer. It is filled with stories and anecdotes to inspire and motivate you in your relationship with Christ.

I pray and hope that you enjoy this adventure as you draw truth from the Word of God for personal transformation, group growth and living out God's purposes in the world!

INTRODUCTION

THE TRUTHFUL REVEALER

Chris Wash, who had dreamed of playing for a top college basketball team, wound up standing on a highway overpass, just waiting for the chance to jump. In the preceding months, reports *Newsweek,* "Wash, a 6-foot-2 guard on the Plano West High School Team in Plano, Texas, went from a rangy 180 pounds to a hulking 230, with shoulders so big he could barely pull on his backpack in the morning. And he developed a whole new personality to match that intimidating physique: depressed, aggressive and volatile" (Jerry Adler, "Toxic Strength," December 20, 2004).

Steroids were the cause of this transformation in Chris. Did he and his fellow students really know the devastating side effects? Not likely. But now the truth is out.

Unfortunately, Wash is not alone. The physical impact and the mood-altering effects of steroids are beginning to make front-page news. Wash's friend Taylor Hooton, a promising young baseball player who also used steroids, was later found dangling from his belt in his bedroom, a tragic suicide.

Recently the truth about steroids and their side effects has been spread all over the media, with all-star major league baseball players at the center of the controversy. Athletes wanted what "roids" could give them—an increase in strength and power in a short period of time. What they ignored, or never knew, was the truth about these anabolic drugs, especially their debilitating side effects.

Some truth is difficult to handle because it runs counter to our desires and expectations. Even when the truth might save our life or protect us from hurting others, we can be stubborn and ignore it. Sometimes, as for these high school athletes, the results can be deadly.

Jesus was committed to the truth. In fact, he claimed to embody truth. Part of his mission was to reveal the truth about himself, about the Father in heaven, about the world, sin, eternal life and what it means to live an abundant life. Each of us must respond to these revelations, for Jesus makes great claims that must be reckoned with.

Let's look at some of the truths Jesus came to show us about God, our past, our needs, our identity, our life's calling and our ultimate destiny. Sometimes his message will be encouraging and comforting; at other points it may be unsettling and challenging. But in every case you will find it engaging. Listen to the Truthful Revealer.

ONE

SHOWS US OUR FATHER

Anyone who has seen me has seen the Father.

☐ GATHERING TO LISTEN

Fathers have a considerable impact on our emotional, physical and spiritual development. A father's power and presence can hold great sway over us. What Chicago Bulls fan can forget the sight of Michael Jordan lying on the floor of the basketball locker room, bawling his eyes out after winning the NBA Championship the year his father died? The loss of his dad—his mentor and idol—was devastating to Jordan. Fans had never known how powerful this relationship was until Jordan collapsed crying that day, NBA trophy in hand.

The movie *Ray*, in which Jamie Foxx plays the famous piano player Ray Charles, depicts a man who struggled with blindness, drugs, infidelity and fame. Later in life he was able to achieve a greater level of emotional and physical stability. But the film makes one thing clear. Ray Robinson—his real name—grew up without a father, so the entire burden of raising a challenging yet promising boy had fallen to a courageous mother. She did well. But one wonders what the impact of a strong, faithful father might have been on this young man.

- Off the top of your head, what are the first words that come to mind when you hear the word *father*?

- The Bible tells us that Jesus came to reveal the Father to us. Most of us already have an idea of what a father is like, based on fathers we know, including our own. But let's look at our images of God. Do you ever wonder, *What kind of father is God?* Perhaps your image of God is similar to your image of earthly fathers. Do any of these words below describe how you view (or once viewed) your heavenly Father? Pick one or two that stand out most and explain why.

powerful	caring	fair
loving	distant	just
fair	firm	truthful
angry	needy	weak
kind	friendly	complacent

☐ **ENCOUNTERING JESUS**

Jesus wants to help people get a clear picture of the Father in heaven. Rather than simply rattling off a list of God's attributes, Jesus uses real situations to describe the nature of the Father.

In the first-century world, many people lived on the fringes of poverty. There was no social security system, no welfare, no job security or insurance benefits, no means of preserving food long term. People lived day to day and often worried about just getting by. Would God take care of them?

Read Matthew 6:25-34.

1. What are some of the causes of worry in your life right now?

2. Summarize Jesus' teaching on why we should not be overly concerned about food, water and clothing. Let's face it, for most of us, these are not "basic" concerns. But we do worry about other things—education for our kids, a warm home, a steady job, medical and drug costs, retirement income. What is Jesus saying about these basic concerns?

3. How do you respond to Jesus' statement, "Do not worry about your life"? Does he sound out of touch with reality, or do his words strike a chord with you?

☐ JOINING THE CONVERSATION

4. Jesus often uses word pictures to make a point or get us to think outside the box. What descriptions of the heavenly Father come to mind as you consider the images Jesus uses here to describe God?

5. What is Jesus saying about how to order our priorities in light of our understanding of the Father?

You may want to read what Jesus says in Matthew 7:9-11 for another perspective on our heavenly Father. Jesus acknowledges that earthly parents are not perfect, but usually, their intentions are good. God, however, is a perfect parent who loves us way more than even the most doting earthly parent ever could.

6. How do you view God's ability to provide what your earthly father could not or did not?

Do you still have doubts about God's provision for your life?

☐ **CONNECTING OUR STORIES**

7. Tell of a recent time when your needs were met unexpectedly, so that you felt blessed. Did you see the Father's hand at work in the situation? Were other people involved in meeting your needs?

8. Consider how your group might be used by the Father to bring care and support to one another. How about people in need outside of the group?

☐ **FINDING OUR WAY**

9. What does it look like, in everyday life, to "seek first [God's] kingdom and his righteousness"? How could you help each other to do that? Use the following exercise to help you. There are no right answers here. These are simply prompts to generate discussion.

Kingdom seekers focus their minds on_____
_____ instead of _____.

Open their hearts to _____
_____instead of hardening their hearts.

Approach each day with an attitude of _____
_____instead of letting _____
attitudes control them.

Keep their eyes fixed on _____
because _____.

Work diligently and serve faithfully knowing that _____
_____.

☐ **PRAYING TOGETHER**

Here are some things you might include in a time of focused prayer.

• Spend some time thanking God for who he is as Father. Be mindful of any anger, resentment or disappointment you might be harboring toward God or others.

- Thank God for your earthly father and the good he brought to your life; forgive him for his failures and honor him for his impact.
- If you are a father, ask God to help you express the love of the heavenly Father to your children.
- Bring your worries to Jesus and ask others to pray with or for you. When we simply name our cares and trust God with them, we find relief and a sense of gratitude for what we have already been given.

TWO

Jesus
DISCLOSES OUR IDENTITY

He calls his own sheep by name.

☐ GATHERING TO LISTEN

Henri Nouwen wrote his classic work *Life of the Beloved* as a response to a seeking friend who wanted to know the answer to this question: what is the essence of the spiritual life? The key to a life of faith, says Nouwen, is embracing the identity God has given us. We are the beloved of God, we are chosen. He writes:

> When I know that I am chosen, I know that I have been seen as a special person. Someone has noticed me in my uniqueness and has expressed a desire to know me, to come closer to me, to love me. When I write to you that, as the Beloved, we are God's chosen ones, I mean that we have been seen by God from all eternity and seen as unique, special, precious beings. . . . From all eternity, long before you were born and became a part of history, you existed in God's heart. Long before your parents admired you, or your friends acknowledged your gifts, or your teachers, colleagues and employ-

ers encouraged you, you were already "chosen." The eyes of love had seen you as precious, as of infinite beauty, as of eternal value.

- Do you think of yourself as "beloved" and "chosen"? Why or why not?

☐ ENCOUNTERING JESUS
Read John 15:1-17.

1. Look at the two ways Jesus describes those who are related to him. Explain what it means to be associated with him in each of these ways: a fruit-bearing branch (verse 5)

a loving friend of Christ (verse 14)

2. What thoughts come to mind as you read that the love Jesus has for you is the same as the love he has for his heavenly Father?

3. The love Jesus describes flows out of a relationship that includes obedience to his commands. Does it seem to you that Jesus is saying that we earn his love? Why or why not?

☐ JOINING THE CONVERSATION

4. Are there people in your life whose favor you have to earn? What are those relationships like?

5. To be chosen *in love* means also to be chosen *for love*—that is, to love others. The one command Jesus is asking us to keep is not simple— to love others as he has loved us (see also John 13:34-35). Take a few moments to reflect on the implications of this command in relation to all of these:

your family

your spouse

your friends

your coworkers

your neighbors

6. Jesus tells us to bear fruit (verse 16). What is this fruit, and what does fruit bearing have to do with our identity as beloved friends of Jesus and lovers of others?

Oswald Chambers, who died in 1917 at the age of forty-three, spent his brief life encouraging many to live in the ways of Jesus. A set of devotional talks given by him from 1915 to 1917 were gathered into My Utmost for His Highest, *which has since remained a bestseller. Among other topics, Chambers reflects on what it means to be chosen by God.*

> *Jesus says, "You did not choose me, but I chose you . . ." (John 15:16). That is the way the grace of God begins. It is a constraint we can never escape; we can disobey it, but we can never start it or produce it ourselves. We are drawn to God by a work of his supernatural grace, and we can never trace back to find where the work began. Our Lord's making of a disciple is supernatural.*

Chambers reminds us that the God of love and grace has chosen us to be his followers and friends. It is his doing, not our earning, that makes this possible. We do not have to perform for him. Those who follow Jesus are chosen in love.

☐ CONNECTING OUR STORIES

7. Many of us have childhood memories of choosing sides or being chosen for a game—some positive, some negative. What was your experience in that situation?

8. How does it feel to be chosen, to be the object of God's love?

☐ FINDING OUR WAY

Jesus laid down his life for his friends when he was nailed to a cross. None of us will ever make a sacrifice as great as his. Yet we are his friends, the objects of his unceasing love. That is our identity as we follow the life and ways of Jesus.

9. What might it look like in this group for us to "lay down our lives for one another" as friends?

10. What would our relationships be like if we embraced our identity as beloved and chosen friends of Jesus and saw others as sharing that identity?

☐ PRAYING TOGETHER

Our identity as beloved friends of God does not mean God winks at our sin. He loves us in spite of our disobedience and our ignorance.

Spend some time reflecting silently and individually about how well you have carried out Christ's command to "love each other as I have loved you." Pray that God would remind you that you are his beloved so you can share that love with others.

Perhaps a time for quiet confession is in order—a moment when you simply agree with God that you have not loved others with the kind of love Jesus has for you. Ask him for power and for the strength to love others, to become less focused on the self.

THREE

Jesus

UNCOVERS OUR HISTORY

He told me everything I ever did.

☐ **GATHERING TO LISTEN**

"Let bygones be bygones." "That's ancient history now; there's no need to talk about it anymore." "Let's not dig up the past." Ever hear statements like these? You have probably said a few of them. They—and others like them—can all be found in *The Handbook of Spiritual Archaeology: Digging Up Everything You Wanted Hidden.* Spiritual archaeology is not a subject you can study in a religion class or on a seminary campus. It is the story of your life, a vivid description (in living color) of all the words, attitudes and decisions you have ever made. On the upside there's the A+ you received in English class and the nice present you gave your mother on Easter. But next to that you'll find the angry outburst at your father and the fuzzy numbers you put on your last sales report. It's all there for close study and scrutiny. There is really only one expert on spiritual archaeology, and that's Jesus. He alone is capable of digging up your entire past.

But unlike the findings of an archaeologist researching the ancient

Near East, these discoveries will never go on display in a museum for the world to view. They are revealed only to us and to God. The only thing we need to decide is what we are going to do with our past. Run from it? Hide it away? Pretend it's not there? Acknowledge only the good stuff? (That's called "selective memory," and it gets better as you get older.)

Our society is fairly mobile, with one in five Americans moving every year. As a result, friendships rarely run deep, and our mobility allows us to run from or conceal our past. Very few people know us and what we've done.

Consider the following questions, and choose one or two to discuss.

- How many of your current friends have known you more than five years? More than ten?

- How many of your high school friends do you still spend time with regularly?

- How many of the people you were friends with ten years ago are you still close to? How about twenty years ago?

- What percentage of your current friends know the key events of your past?

- Would it make you uncomfortable if they knew the details of your life story?

☐ **ENCOUNTERING JESUS**

Read Luke 7:36-50.

1. Jesus' relationship with the Pharisees was often tense and confrontational. You would expect, therefore, that this religious leader had an ulterior motive for inviting Jesus to dinner. Consider some possible motives, listed below, and share your thoughts with the group.

   - He wants to trap Jesus.

   - He is looking for Jesus' weakness.

- He is hoping Jesus will teach heresy.
- He is interested in seeing Jesus up close.
- He wants to be the center of attention.
- He has some personal questions for Jesus.
- He wants to make sure Jesus knows who is in control.
- He wants to humiliate Jesus.
- He is interested in displaying his wealth and power to others.

2. Now look at the woman. What kind of a past do you think she has had?

3. Each of us has a public past and a private past, or you might say we have a "known history" and an "unknown history." In the case of this woman, there is much overlap between the two. In any case, she does not try to hide her past from Jesus. Why not?

4. It was common at formal meals in larger homes to allow people from the community to drop in. After all, there were no movie theaters or coffee shops. Sometimes poetry was read, songs were performed, and other entertainment was offered after the meal. But this woman is unwelcome. What do you think motivates her to overcome her embarrassment and shame and make an appearance?

☐ JOINING THE CONVERSATION

5. Imagine being this woman. Luke tells us that she has lived in a pattern of sin for most of her life. Would you have the courage to do what this woman does? How would you feel if you were her?

6. Jesus is able to reveal the truth about people without shaming them. How does this influence your image of Jesus and how he views your own past?

☐ CONNECTING OUR STORIES

7. Simon neglects basic hospitality (water for feet, oil for head) in his home for Jesus. This would have been a way to honor him and show him respect. What are subtle ways that followers of Jesus neglect to show him honor or hospitality today?

8. As Jesus tells the story of the two debtors in verses 41-42, what emotions do you feel?

How do you respond to the actions of the creditor?

9. Take a moment to be brutally honest. Do you think you would respond to Jesus more as Simon the Pharisee does or as the sinful woman does? Explain what influences your response.

☐ **FINDING OUR WAY**

10. When Jesus uncovers our past, especially those parts that we are not very proud of, what gift does he offer?

How do you respond to this gift?

11. What does this suggest about what we can offer one another in light of Jesus' example?

☐ PRAYING TOGETHER

Consider again the short parable Jesus tells in verses 41-42. Think about the spiritual "debts" of your past. Spend some time praying individually, asking Jesus to gently but truthfully show you the truth about your past and how he views it. Then pray as a group, thanking him for canceling your debt of sin and expressing gratitude and love toward him for his gracious gift.

If you are not certain that Jesus has canceled your debt, or you still feel unworthy to have your past forgiven, or you do not yet feel ready to receive this gift from Christ, you might speak to your group leader or another group member about your feelings. Pray together and ask God to show himself to you.

FOUR

EXPOSES OUR NEEDS

The Son of Man came to seek and to save what was lost.

☐ GATHERING TO LISTEN

I just had my first root canal. It was a procedure I had avoided for several months. The tooth had a crown on it, and I had thought the pain was coming from the crown. At first I had ignored the tooth, hoping the pain would just go away. But every time I drank something cold or closed my teeth on something hard, a vivid reminder emanated from my lower jaw. Taking painkillers, hoping it would heal by itself, and even chewing on the other side would not do the trick.

My dentist confirmed that it was not the crown but the root down under, and I was going to need a root canal. There was a problem deep within my tooth, and no amount of surface-level work was going to fix it. We had to get at the root—literally—of the problem.

Our culture is obsessed with image management, with surface-level beauty and accomplishments. We'd rather ignore what is under the surface, especially if it is uncomfortable or painful. So we resort to extreme makeovers and pain management strategies. What we really need is a kind of spiritual root canal—an uncomfortable procedure, but one that will cure what lies beneath.

God knows we have a deeper problem, and therefore he has given us a more lasting solution. We have a sin problem—painful to admit, yet impossible to manage on our own. We need help. When we acknowledge we need help and admit our inadequacy, we are drawn closer to God. We need his grace, love and tender forgiveness.

- Have you ever ignored a problem or situation, hoping it would go away but knowing it would only get worse if neglected? What happened over the course of time?

☐ ENCOUNTERING JESUS

Read Mark 2:1-12.

1. At times Jesus enjoys great popularity, while other times he seems to be the object of people's wrath and anger. What do you notice about the way people respond to Jesus in this account?

2. How would you describe the attitudes of the four young men who bring their paralyzed friend to Jesus? What are they seeking from Jesus?

3. From what Jesus says to the paralyzed man, what does Jesus seem to think the man needs?

□ JOINING THE CONVERSATION

4. What was the first thing Jesus notices about the paralytic and his friends (see verse 5)?

5. Place yourself in the story for a moment. What may be going through the minds of people who are present? Look at the list below, choose a person or group, and imagine what they might be thinking.

   • the owner of the house

   • people who knew Jesus well

   • those on the outside looking in

   • people in the home listening to his teaching

   • the four young friends

   • the boy on the mat

   • the teachers of the law

6. Jesus exposes some needs here—the needs of a young paralytic and the needs of the Pharisees and teachers of the law. Explain what each needs.

7. It is apparent that spiritual and physical needs of people are somehow interrelated. If this is true, what does this imply for how we view others and ourselves?

There is nothing like felt inadequacy to help me depend solely on God. What is sin but not living up to your potential, not being all that God calls you to be? . . . Feeling in your guts your powerlessness without God is an important part of coming to union with God. Nothing can so enable you to feel your own powerlessness as to finally be able to own your sin and embrace it as Jesus did on the cross.

MACRINA WIEDERKEHR, **A Tree Full of Angels**

☐ CONNECTING OUR STORIES

8. The paralytic and his friends think he needs to be cured of his physical ailments. But Jesus sees a different need. Tell of a physical need you have right now (for example, a better job, a new house or a better relationship with your spouse).

Is it possible that your deepest need may not be the one you first think of? Why is this?

9. Imagine yourself in the place of the paralytic. Perhaps he feels embarrassed about his physical condition, even more so when his friends create this dramatic entry into the house where Jesus is teaching. How do you think he feels when Jesus looks at him and says, "Your sins are forgiven"?

☐ **FINDING OUR WAY**

10. The paralytic has to trust his friends to bring him to Jesus. His needs are exposed in front of those friends. What steps can you take together to make your group environment a safe place for your needs to be exposed to the tender love and healing of Jesus?

☐ **PRAYING TOGETHER**

Not only does Jesus expose our deepest need for healing and forgiveness, but he is ultimately the only one who can meet those needs. Pray about your own neediness. Imagine that Jesus is standing before you. He addresses you by name and asks, "What do you need?" He knows what you need, but go ahead and verbalize it. Ask him to help you see the real need behind what you think you need. Then spend some time thanking him for not only seeing and caring about your needs but meeting them as well.

FIVE

UNVEILS OUR DESTINY

I go to prepare a place for you.

☐ GATHERING TO LISTEN

In his bestselling book *The Purpose-Driven Life,* pastor Rick Warren writes:

> You were made for a mission. God is at work in the world, and he wants you to join him. This assignment is called your mission. God wants you to have both a ministry in the Body of Christ and a mission in the world. . . . Our English word *mission* comes from the Latin word for "sending." Being a Christian includes being sent into the world as a representative of Jesus Christ. Jesus said, *"As the Father has sent me, I am sending you."*
>
> Jesus clearly understood his life mission on earth. At age twelve he said, *"I must be about my Father's business,"* and twenty-one years later, dying on the cross, he said, *"It is finished."* Like bookends, these two statements frame a well-lived, purpose-driven life. Jesus completed the mission the Father gave him. . . .
>
> Fulfilling your life mission on earth is an essential part of living for God's glory.

- Do you agree or disagree with Warren's ideas? How are the ideas of
  mission and destiny connected in your mind?

☐ ENCOUNTERING JESUS

In John 13, Jesus tells his disciples that someone will betray him, that he
will be leaving them to go to a place they cannot come, that Peter will
disown him three times. Their confusion is evident in John 13:36-37.

Read John 14:1-7.

1. Then Jesus says, "Do not let your hearts be troubled." What do you
   suppose the disciples are thinking as they hear Jesus' words?

2. Where does Jesus say he is going? What do his plans tell us about our
   ultimate destiny?

3. Jesus doesn't reveal all the details about his leaving but asks his disciples to trust him. Have you ever had to trust someone even when
   you didn't know the details of their plans? How did that feel?

☐ **JOINING THE CONVERSATION**

4. In verse 4, Jesus tells the disciples that they know "the way" to where
    he is going. Thomas, famous for his doubts and questions, wonders
    how this can be. How does Jesus answer him? (See verse 6.)

    What do you think Jesus means by this reply?

5. Consider Jesus' claim that he is the way, truth and life. What does this
    say about him?

    Do you think he is arrogant in making this claim? Why or why not?

☐ **CONNECTING OUR STORIES**

6. Recall a time you were lost and could not find your way. How did you
    eventually get to where you wanted to go? Did you have help?

7. Jesus talks about trust and about finding the way to God. How are
    these two ideas related?

8. What is your biggest barrier when it comes to trusting God, especially when things are difficult?

☐ **FINDING OUR WAY**

9. What do you think Jesus is revealing to us about the ultimate destiny of those who follow him?

What steps do you need to take to claim that destiny?

10. How can we help each other find "the way, the truth and the life"? Where are you on your spiritual journey?

- seeking answers about Jesus
- following the ways of Jesus but confused about some things
- committed to the ways of Jesus and wanting others to encounter him
- wandering away from Jesus for a season because of disappointment, fear and frustration
- ambivalent about Jesus at this point; just listening and watching

☐ **PRAYING TOGETHER**

Pray that God would show each person in the group the next step they need to take to claim their destiny and receive what Jesus wants to give them.

SIX

CLARIFIES OUR CALLING

Don't be afraid; from now on
you will be [a fisherman] "catching" people.

☐ GATHERING TO LISTEN

Author and educator Parker Palmer writes in *Let Your Life Speak*, "Vocation does not mean a goal that I pursue. It means a calling that I hear." Do you feel that you have a calling in life—a purpose or a mission? Is Jesus calling you to a certain vocation or a certain place of service? This doesn't necessarily mean a calling to go into professional ministry. He may be calling you to be a doctor, a plumber, a business leader or a construction worker. Whatever your vocation, seek to do it well, in a way that honors God and the way he designed each of us.

This sounds good. But how can we determine what that looks like? And does calling just involve our work life? We must listen to God, taking note of how he made us and what stirs our passions. In the company of Jesus we find a friend who notices who we truly are and seeks to release us to our God-given calling.

- Talk about whether you sense you are living according to your calling now.

☐ ENCOUNTERING JESUS

Imagine the scene in the passage we are going to read: Jesus is standing on the beach, giving a talk. Nearby, some fishermen have just finished their night's work and are cleaning their nets as they listen. The normally quiet shore is crowded with people who want to hear Jesus. The fishermen were already there and probably hadn't expected a gathering of onlookers. They're likely tired from fishing till dawn and are wondering why this rabbi and his followers are there. Yet Jesus draws them in and engages them by asking if he can sit in their boat, a few feet from shore, in order to address the crowd.

Read Luke 5:1-11.

1. What do you think is going through Simon's mind as he listens to Jesus?

2. Look through this story and list, in order, the things Jesus asks Simon to do. What do you notice?

How is Jesus building a relationship with Simon by making these requests of him?

3. Notice Simon's response to Jesus' request in verse 5. What attitudes do you see in Simon?

How does his attitude change in the course of the story?

4. Simon uses the word *Master* and does what Jesus asks "because you say so." What does this tell you about who Simon is and who he understands Jesus to be?

☐ JOINING THE CONVERSATION

5. Have you ever felt unworthy or uncomfortable in the presence of someone you considered "holy" or more mature than you? Talk about how you felt and how you related to this person.

6. What caused Simon to say the words recorded in verse 8?

7. How do you think this encounter with Jesus influenced Simon and the other fishermen to follow Jesus?

What does the story tell us about how Jesus calls us?

☐ **CONNECTING OUR STORIES**

8. Simon Peter is gripped with fear when he realizes that Jesus is more than a teacher to respect—he is a Master to revere. How does Jesus confront this fear?

9. Have you ever felt that God was calling you to do something, but you were afraid of God or afraid of what he might ask of you?

☐ **FINDING OUR WAY**

10. How is the calling of every follower of Jesus similar to the calling of Simon Peter, James and John?

How is it different?

11. Jesus brings great clarity to the life mission of these men—to "catch" people for the kingdom. What is your life mission?

12. Is it important to you that your life mission relates to what God is doing in the world?

☐ **PRAYING TOGETHER**

Pray for each other, that you would each hear God's calling with clarity and would have the courage to obey it. God's call concerns participation in his work, not necessarily as a vocation (though some are called into full-time ministry). Pray for clarity about how to connect your everyday activities and life with the call and purposes of God in this world. Pray for focus, so you will be aware of opportunities to connect people to the teachings and ways of Jesus.

NOTES FOR LEADERS

Each session has a similar format using the components below. Here is a very rough guide for the amount of time you might spend on each segment for a ninety-minute meeting time, excluding additional social time. This is a general guide, and you will learn to adjust the format as you become comfortable working together as a group:

Gathering to Listen	5-10 minutes
Encountering Jesus	15 minutes
Joining the Conversation	20 minutes
Connecting Our Stories	20 minutes
Finding Our Way	10 minutes
Praying Together	about 10 minutes

You can take some shortcuts or take longer as the group decides, but strive to stay on schedule for a ninety-minute meeting including prayer time. You will also want to save time to attend to personal needs and prayer. This will vary by group and can also be accomplished in personal relationships you develop between meetings.

As group leader, know that you help create an environment for spiritual growth. Here are a few things to consider as you invite people to follow in the company of Jesus.

LEADER TIPS

Practice authenticity and truth telling. Do not pretend an elephant is not sitting in the middle of the room when everyone knows it is.

- Does your group have a commitment to pursue personal change and growth?
- Set some ground rules or a covenant for group interactions. Consider values like confidentiality, respect and integrity.
- Model and encourage healthy self-disclosure through icebreakers, storytelling and getting to know one another between meetings.

CONNECTING SEEKERS TO JESUS

This simple process is designed to help you guide a person toward commitment to Christ. It is only a guide, intended to give you the feel of a conversation you might have.

1. Describe what you see going on. "Mike, I sense you are open to knowing Jesus more personally. Is this the case?"

2. Affirm that Jesus is always inviting people to follow him (John 6:35-40). "Mike, Jesus has opened the door to a full and dynamic relationship with him. All who believe in Jesus are welcome. Do you want to place your trust in Jesus?"

3. Describe how sin has separated us from God, making a relationship with God impossible (Romans 3:21-26). "Though Jesus desires fellowship with us, our sin stands in the way. So Jesus went to the cross to pay for that sin, to take away the guilt of that sin and to make reconciliation with God possible again. Are you aware that your sin has become a barrier between you and Jesus?"

4. Show how Jesus' death on the cross bridged the gap between us and God (Romans 5:1-11). "Now we can have peace with God, a relationship with Jesus, because his death canceled out our sin debt. All our offenses against God are taken away by Jesus."

5. Invite them to have a brief conversation with God (2 Corinthians 5:11—6:2). "By asking for his forgiveness and being reconnected to Jesus, we can have new life, one that starts now. Jesus invites you to join him in this new life—to love him, learn his ways, connect to his people and trust in his purposes. We can talk to him now and express that desire if you want to."

These five suggestions are designed to create a dialogue and discern if a person wants to follow Jesus. Points to remember:

1. Keep dialogue authentic and conversational.
2. God is at work here—you are simply a guide, leading someone toward a step of faith in Jesus.
3. The heart is more important than the specific words.
4. People will not understand all that Christ has done, so don't try to confuse them with too much information.
5. Keep it simple.
6. Don't put words in someone's mouth. Let them describe how they want to follow Jesus and participate in his life.

7. Use Scripture as needed. You may recite some or let them read the passages.
8. Remember, this is not a decision to join an organization. It is a relationship with a person, an invitation to a new life and a new community: "Come follow me."

As the person expresses the desire to follow Jesus, encourage them to read the Gospel of Mark and discover the life of Jesus and his teachings more clearly.

SESSION 1.
JESUS SHOWS US OUR FATHER.
Matthew 6:25-34

Gathering to Listen (8-10 minutes). For some this may be a painful exercise. Be compassionate. Often people have mixed feelings about their family of origin. Someone might describe their earthly father with words like *demanding, loving* and *hardworking,* showing such ambivalence. If someone seems to have unresolved issues, this is not the place to try to fix or even do therapy. Just listen, let people free associate.

Those who have a more positive view of their earthly father will have an easier time imagining a loving and generous heavenly Father. When Jesus uses the image of Father, he's not saying that God is like an earthly father in every way. In fact, he sometimes contrasts what earthly, sinful fathers do with what the perfect heavenly Father does (see Matthew 7:9-11).

Many people will tend to see God as being like their earthly father, but some do not. This is a time to help people see how they view God and to begin thinking why that is. Is their view informed by the Bible or by experience? Do they place expectations on God that he does not meet?

Again, we are not trying to do any deep therapy here or get into "father blaming." But there is truth to the idea that our image of God can be colored by the image we have of our earthly dad.

Encountering Jesus (15 minutes). Remember that this passage is in the Sermon on the Mount. The Sermon is more than a random collection of topical messages from Jesus on a variety of subjects (worry, prayer, divorce, adultery, etc.). It is a message about the kingdom of God and what kingdom living looks like. Jesus, the King, is on the scene, and his kingdom life is present and available to all who seek it (Matthew 7:7-8).

Granted, Jesus was an itinerant preacher, and there were no CDs or TVs, so his messages were given repeatedly and often. In a culture that relied on oral communication, Jesus' illustrations and pithy sayings were memorable and repeatable. It may be that Matthew organized his teachings into one "sermon" but it actually took place over several days and was repeated in other locations.

As we come to the issue of worrying, Jesus is not giving us "five simple steps to overcome worry," such as we might find in the self-help section of the bookstore. Rather, he is giving a kingdom perspective on the nature of the Father and how he interacts with his creatures. If people want to know what that looks like, they can just look at Jesus.

The focus here should be on verse 32: your heavenly Father knows what you need. He will take care of you. It is because of his care that we need not worry. Worry is a form of fear, and fear is the opposite of love. Perfect love casts out fear (see 1 John 4:18). We want participants to begin to grasp the incredible love of God, the Father who knows their needs and provides for them.

Though we are not doing a full Bible study on the topic of worry, it is a major theme of Jesus' illustration and exhortation in this text. Stress the process rather than the end result: if you are a chronic worrier, you're not going to change overnight. Try to get at the fear that is behind the worry, and focus on what is true about our heavenly Father as an antidote to worry. The solution is a relationship, not a set of rules. When children are afraid, they run to the arms of their parents, not to a book. Encourage group members to talk about how they feel, knowing that their heavenly Father knows their needs.

Joining the Conversation (20 minutes). Some people may have trouble connecting with the word pictures of birds and flowers—they may seem disconnected from real life in urban America. One version of the Bible tells us to "consider" the birds, though, and you may want to encourage your group to do just that. To "consider" means to take notice and even meditate on something. If you watch birds, you will notice they don't sit in their nests waiting for God to feed them. They hop and fly around looking for food—for crumbs, insects, worms. Our Father does not want to turn us into spiritual trust-fund babies. He wants us to join him in his work. These verses are not an excuse to just sit back and make no effort, waiting for God to serve us. Trust requires action. Setting priorities in line with kingdom values is the focus. If God has provided us with life and a body, will he not also provide things of lesser worth like clothes and food? But trust is the challenge—easier said than done. Don't be afraid to press the group about what each person (including you) seems to put trust in every day—other people, money, status, relationships, job "security," and so on.

Connecting Our Stories (20 minutes). Most often God works through people. Our temptation may be to attribute the help we receive to the efforts of others, not necessarily to God. Prompt group members to look for God in every instance of provision. He is often behind the scenes, working his purposes through what may appear to be rather ordinary means. Remember that Jesus tapped twelve very ordinary (and often rebellious) men to be his core group. It should not surprise us that God takes pleasure in working through his creation and in harmony with it.

If participants are able to see that God has put other people in their lives to provide care and love, then it follows that God may want to use them in someone else's life to do the same. Challenge group members to be available as agents of God's grace and love.

Finding Our Way (10 minutes). The emphasis here should be priorities and focus. As seekers of God's kingdom we reorient our lives around God's purposes, trusting him as our heavenly Father. So though there are no set answers, you might emphasize that kingdom seekers "focus their minds on eternal things" instead of temporary things, on "people" instead of "stuff," and so on. Kingdom seekers open their hearts to the poor, to God's work, to the work of the Holy Spirit in them, to people searching for answers, to people in need. They approach each day with an attitude of "Whatever you want me to do, God," instead of an attitude of self-centeredness.

Kingdom seekers fix their eyes on the life and ways of Jesus because he has modeled and taught what kingdom living looks like. And they work hard because of the rewards promised to those who are faithful.

Those are the kinds of responses we hope to see, though there could be a broad range of ideas. Do not judge answers; simply ask questions to clarify and guide the group to engage with one another.

Praying Together (about 10 minutes). A few different options are provided for focusing the prayer time. These are only suggestions—feel free to add your own.

SESSION 2.
JESUS DISCLOSES OUR IDENTITY.
John 15:1-17

Gathering to Listen (3-5 minutes). Encourage people to examine their own identity. To be the beloved does not mean just that a particular someone loves you but that your primary identity is "the beloved." It comes from an awareness of God's love for us. It does not come and go with our feelings; it is at the core of who we are. God's love of us is unrelenting and inexhaustible.

Encountering Jesus (20 minutes). Jesus' love, and our return of that love, develops into intimacy with him. Remind participants that Jesus is the initiator in the relationship—that our identity comes from his loving us, not our efforts to earn his love back. He is the lover, and we are the object of his affection. See Romans 5:8.

In verse 5 Jesus calls us branches. Those who are connected to him bear fruit. Branches not connected to him do not bear fruit. Using the analogy of a vineyard, Jesus explains that dead branches are useless and thrown into the fire. Here Jesus is talking about productivity in the Christian life. The analogy helps us grasp the importance of staying connected to him in deep relationship. If we do not, our lives cannot bear the fruit of his work in us; we shrivel up. We are like a branch that gets disconnected from the vine: it dries up and ceases to serve the purpose for which it was created. It produces no life that others can benefit from and enjoy. So what good is it now? Only firewood. That is sad. Vine branches were designed to bring forth grapes, not to be burned as firewood. How better to be a branch yielding grapes (life) to be tasted and enjoyed. The vineyard owner, God, removes the dead wood from his church, unproductive lives that are not producing fruit. The assumption is they are not connected to Christ in any vital way and therefore serve no purpose in God's kingdom.

Obedience and joy are the natural outputs of fruitful people connected to the life of Jesus. We are not earning the love of Jesus. Jesus is talking instead about the natural outcomes of a relationship. Those who love him obey him. We "remain" in his love if we obey him. If we disobey, we do not remain in his love. Notice it does *not* say that he no longer loves us. His love is constant; but whether we remain in it depends on the nature and quality of our connection with Jesus.

Joining the Conversation (20 minutes). Though we cannot earn God's favor, we can earn the favor of people. And we can fall from grace, as it were, with people. Where we once were a hero, we may quickly become a heel. Now we are the rejected one because we have disappointed the other. This is not true with God. Though our disobedience displeases and angers him, it never quenches his love. Disobedience elicits discipline, not rejection.

Friendships that require us to constantly earn favor become performance-oriented relationships. "What have you done for me lately?" is the defining question. With God, we are constantly reminded of what he has done for us. And that evokes love and obedience.

Seekers may not understand this. It is hard to accept and believe unconditional love. The fear that they cannot earn favor with God or that they have fallen so far from grace that they can never return may be the biggest obstacle to a seeker's embrace of God. Be aware of any such viewpoints in the group, and encourage everyone to pursue a close relationship with God through Jesus, whose love is not measured by our performance.

As members reflect on how to show love to others, remind them that we are not trying to outperform anyone. Rather, we are trying to show how the love of Christ overflows from us into the lives of people we know. Such relationships should be marked by God's love and the friendship of Jesus.

The fruit in verse 16 would be similar to the fruit of the Spirit in Galatians 5:22-23: love, joy, peace and so on characterize those who are connected to Jesus, the vine. Growth in character, renewed compassion for the poor and love for justice permeate the heart of a follower of Christ.

Connecting Our Stories (20 minutes). Some may recall painful memories, so be sensitive. Even if they were not chosen first for dodgeball, point out that most people have been chosen for something: when they found a spouse or were hired for a job. Urge group members to think about being chosen in activities other than sports: perhaps for an honors class or as a finalist in an art or music competition. Nonetheless, there may be some who have felt a strong sense of rejection at home, in relationships or at work. This is why it is so important to know that we are chosen by God in Christ.

Yet awareness of being chosen by God can be an awkward feeling. Some may not feel "chosen" because they are not yet Christ-followers. It is important to note here that there are many things we were all chosen for:

1. For life—each of us has breath and a life to live, given to us by God. We did not earn it.

2. For this small group—each person was "chosen" or invited to be a member, with little regard for past history or religious expertise.

3. For the gift of redemption—each of us is offered hope and forgiveness in Christ. Jesus was called "the Lamb of God who takes away the sin of the world," which means his death is for everyone. The question is whether we will receive and appropriate that gift of God in humble repentance and submission (see John 1:12; 3:16; 5:24; 6:40, 47-51; 10:27-30; 11:25-27; 14:6).

Finding Our Way (10 minutes). These questions are designed to help members share the love of Christ with others. Focus on the practical aspects of living out our identity as ones who are loved. To lay down our lives means a level of sacrifice, of counting others as more important than ourselves. This affects our relationships, our attitudes and our behavior toward one another and toward the world around us.

It is rare that we would ever be in a situation to actually give our physical life for someone, but we are often called to lay down our agenda, to let go of what we have assumed is most important, to help someone else. Encourage group members to think about how they can be loving and unselfish.

Praying Together (about 10 minutes). To know we are the beloved does not give us an inflated sense of self-importance. Rather, it is humbling and inspiring to know that God has chosen us. Hopefully, it inspires us to share that love with the people around us. God's love does not get used up, it is not a limited commodity. The more it is shared, the more of it there is, available to more and more people.

SESSION 3.
JESUS UNCOVERS OUR HISTORY.
Luke 7:36-50

Gathering to Listen (5 minutes). By asking some of these questions, we simply want to highlight that mobility encourages us to shrink back from deep relationships. Because of this mobility in our society, it's easy to conceal our past or to try to run from it. We think we leave our past behind when we move, but really we carry it wherever we go, even if others do not know our story.

You do not have to make this a deep time of personal examination. Be aware, though, that the questions here may stir up some troubled thoughts and emotions in members. Someone left behind a broken relationship, and it was never reconciled. Someone else left behind an opportunity when their spouse landed a dream job, and they resent having lost it. Or these questions may simply cause a few people to laugh at how often we move on, especially compared to people of other cultures.

Encountering Jesus (15 minutes). While there is no need to spend much time guessing Simon's motives for inviting Jesus to his house, his actions and his thoughts reveal that he may not have had Jesus' best interests in mind. The Pharisees often questioned Jesus, trying to figure out what he was up to. They felt threatened by him. In this story, Simon's personal story—his true motives—are exposed, and we discover who he really is.

Relationships do that to us. The more we spend time with each other, the more we discover about one another, both good and not so good. This is the challenge of building community as a group. Will we love and embrace one another as we encounter differences and quirks? Or do we want pseudocommunity, where we put on masks and hide our true self, hoping others will like us?

The woman's past is apparently common knowledge in the little town, so it's likely that her sin was very public. She was probably a prostitute, or at least her sexual conduct fell outside the norms of marriage. Luke tells us she had not just occasionally sinned but had "lived a sinful life." Of course, we have all done that—lived lives filled with sinful actions and decisions. For many of us those sins are unknown to those around us. We are basically good neighbors, loving parents, helpful friends. But that does not mean we have a sinless life.

The woman—whose name is a mystery—came specifically to see Jesus, having entered the home during a meal at which many guests were present. The Pharisee was likely wealthy, for poorer people did not have couches or tables as we know them today. It was the custom to open up larger homes at or after meals to create a sense of community and to entertain guests. Apparently this woman came in right at the beginning of the meal, which probably shocked the guests a bit. Given her past, she would not have been expected to attend at all, let alone coming as soon as Jesus arrived. Perhaps she had followed him down the street, knowing he would attend the meal and party at this home.

By New Testament times the triclinium was in use: a grouping of three tables in a horseshoe or U-shaped arrangement, with couches on one side of the tables, leaving an opening in the middle for servants to enter bringing food and drinks. Guests reclined on these short couches with their head toward the food and their feet hanging off the back. This made it easy for their feet to be washed even as they talked and ate. In this case it allowed the sinful woman to kneel at Jesus' feet and wipe them with her tears and hair.

Joining the Conversation (20 minutes). The woman doesn't try to hide her past. She enters the dinner party and starts crying. Perhaps her shame and fear evoke such emotion. Or perhaps she has seen the relentless tenderness of Jesus in action and has pinned her hopes on his mercy and grace. She knows she can't hide who she is. And Jesus doesn't try to hide it either. But while he doesn't wink at her sin, he holds her up as an example to Simon, whose sin of self-righteous pride is also revealed in the conversation with Jesus.

It takes great courage and faith to step into the arms of Jesus. You discover he knows everything about you and yet has everything to offer. The woman has such courage because she has a clear picture of who she is. More important, she has a clear picture of who Jesus is.

Connecting Our Stories (20 minutes). None of Simon's servants had washed the feet of Jesus or offered him oil to refresh his face. The customary Middle Eastern greeting—a kiss—had not been given to Jesus, though he was the honored guest. This was probably intentional (see verses 44-46), designed to humiliate him socially. The servants should have attended to him immediately, but instead the woman took on their role.

Help group members to see how they may be a little like Simon, taking Jesus' presence for granted or treating him with a casualness bordering on disrespect. Or perhaps we have an agenda for Jesus and want to use him to benefit ourselves. We may not want to expose or embarrass him, but perhaps we want him to solve our problems, fix our kids, give us a promotion or remove an irritating person from our life. It's all about us. Instead, our attention and affections should be directed at him.

Do we really give him the honor he deserves? Or do we think we are doing him a favor by even talking to him?

Finding Our Way (10 minutes). When Jesus uncovers our sinful history, he offers forgiveness—if we ask for it. Group members may notice that Jesus uncovers Simon's sin of pride and self-righteousness but never seems to offer him forgiveness. Simon, though he acknowledges the point of Jesus' parable, doesn't take the next step of seeking forgiveness. When Jesus uncovers our history, our response should be like that of the woman: to ask for forgiveness.

It is important that your small group environment provide acceptance, grace and forgiveness. If there are non-Christians in the group, do not expect them to abide by biblical standards for living, and do not require they adopt those standards as non-Christians. Meet them where they are. Let the power of community, the teaching of the Holy Spirit and the truth of the Bible do their work. Your job is to create an environment of trust and hope. Would the sinful woman be received into your group?

Praying Together (about 10 minutes). If there are group members who have not yet accepted Christ as their forgiver, be sensitive to that. However, doing this "moral inventory" may be a helpful step on their journey toward faith. Remind all participants that this self-examination exercise is not about shame but about truth telling, which leads to love and forgiveness, which ultimately leads to freedom.

Do not push people to disclose specifics of their past sins. Rather, stress that nothing can separate us from God's love, and all he asks is that we acknowledge our past and allow him to heal it.

SESSION 4.
JESUS EXPOSES OUR NEEDS.
Mark 2:1-12

Gathering to Listen (5 minutes). To set up the discussion, this question is designed to help people realize that there are deeper issues and problems in the spiritual life, just as there are in the physical life. Neglecting deeper issues means ignoring what may lie at the root of our struggles and disconnection from God.

Encountering Jesus (15 minutes). Our neediness draws us to God. Jesus exposes our needs but does not simply leave us there—he also meets them. If we are willing to have them exposed, that is, to embrace our failures and our sin and say, "Yes, this is the truth about me," then we open ourselves up to a truthful encounter with Jesus Christ.

In this passage Jesus returns home to Capernaum, probably to the home of Peter and Andrew, his base of operation in Galilee (see Mark 1:29). This small, one-room structure was typical of the homes of peasants. The roof was flat, supported with wooden beams and made of thatch and compacted earth. Sometimes tiles were included in this structure. It is likely that our four adventurers pulled up the tiles, then dug away at the thatch and compacted soil, causing dirt and grass to come crumbling upon those inside the home. They made quite an entrance. This took persistence and determination, evidence of their faith.

We know that the paralytic was young because of the Greek word used when Jesus addresses him in verse 5 as "son." This word is also translated "child" or "young man." Focus discussion on the hearts and attitudes of these four young men and their paralyzed friend. Encourage members to remember times when they were young and did outrageous things to get somewhere. Young people will sit in the rain for hours to get concert tickets, hitchhike across the country, or pile in a car with five others (all with fifteen dollars in their pockets!) to drive to Florida for spring break. The young people in this account are just as "foolish" but have a higher purpose in mind.

Very few people we read about in the Gospels feel neutral about Jesus. They love him and crowd around, or they hate him. He triggers a strong reaction, because people are unable to pretend very long—he sees their thoughts, exposes their needs.

Joining the Conversation (20 minutes). Jesus notices the faith of these young people, yet he has never talked with them. Their actions demonstrate their faith. James, referring to the faith of Abraham, says, "You see that his faith and actions were working together, and his faith was made complete by what he did" (James 2:22). Faith without works is indeed dead. Many listening to Jesus teach inside the house "believe" things about him, but these young people put their faith in action.

Each person here responds to Jesus differently, so ask the group to really get into the story and imagine the situation. Use these people and groups as a way of helping everyone understand the moment. It really sheds light on the story.

• The owners of the home are likely Peter and Andrew, or Peter's mother-in-law. They probably never rest when Jesus is around!

- People who know Jesus well may be trying to use their relationship with him to gain favor or feel important.
- Those on the outside looking in probably feel detached, having to rely on secondhand information about what is going on inside.
- People in the home listening to his teaching are likely shocked as the roof crumbles above them. Some may be indignant at such an interruption (after all, they have front-row seats to see Jesus!).
- The four young friends are likely hopeful and determined, and perhaps a bit reckless. Who knows, the roof could collapse!
- The young man on the mat must be partially optimistic and yet terrified. Will he feel like a fool if Jesus does not heal him? Will he have to carry this embarrassment with him along with his paralysis?
- The teachers of the law have come from miles around just to see Jesus, probably to trap him with their legal minds and religious training.

Now notice Jesus' response to the situation. It is almost funny. People have just dug away roof tiles and thatch to lower a man into the room, and what Jesus notices is not the interruption or the disturbance but their faith. He sees through the circumstances to the heart of the matter.

He also sees through the teachers of the law, the religious elite who have gathered with the crowd but are second-guessing Jesus' every move. The Pharisees and teachers don't think of themselves as needing anything; they are self-righteous and accusatory. But through his questions Jesus also exposes their need—which is to see the truth and let go of their pride.

Connecting Our Stories (20 minutes). Basically, Jesus is noting that this young man, like all of us, is a sinner. When we are exposed, at first we feel embarrassed. It's likely that the paralyzed man feels embarrassed and uncertain, at least at first. Perhaps he's wishing he hadn't let his overenthusiastic friends talk him into this stunt. Encourage the group to imagine themselves as fellow paralytics, totally dependent on others for everything from eating and drinking to personal hygiene. How does that feel?

When the truth is finally exposed and sins are uncovered, the end result is amazement, joy and praise of God. Jesus has exposed the man's need and provided healing for him—at every level.

Finding Our Way (10 minutes). How can group members bring one another to Jesus? This should prompt discussion about how we pray for each other. This is also an opportunity for a checkup regarding the dynamics of the group. Does it feel safe? Is there an acceptance that allows people to feel okay even as Jesus exposes their neediness? If not, what things in the group need to change?

Praying Together (about 10 minutes). This type of prayer pushes us to "get real" with our needs and our faith. If you imagine Jesus asking you what you need, you have to confront any secret doubt. Do you truly believe that he cares about your needs? Do you actually trust him to meet those needs?

SESSION 5.
JESUS UNVEILS OUR DESTINY.
John 14:1-7

Gathering to Listen (5 minutes). The believer's ultimate destiny is in the presence of Jesus in heaven, but between now and then our destiny is to discover where God is at work and join him in that work. Allow participants to explore the tension between their mission on earth and their ultimate destiny of life with God in eternity. Do seekers in the group understand the Christ-follower's mission and destiny?

Encountering Jesus (20 minutes). Urge group members to try to identify with the disciples' confusion. The major theme is trust, especially when things seem difficult or confusing. Jesus' followers were grappling with the chaos of Jesus' last days. There had been many disappointments and events they didn't understand. The questions should help participants wrestle with the tension between our ultimate destiny (heaven) and our destiny or mission on earth—to trust God and obey him (walk in the Way).

Jesus is using a metaphor of homes and places, things people could see in their mind and understand in their heart. In that time many people had a small home or rented quarters. A personal place prepared by Jesus would be a comforting promise. Jesus is saying he will provide for his followers—we need not be afraid of our final destination. And as for numbers, "God's house" has many "rooms," more than enough for all. In Near Eastern and Middle Eastern culture it was (and still is) not unusual for sons and daughters to have a room or apartment in the home of parents, even after their marriage. So the imagery communicates that the Father will not leave his children homeless.

Joining the Conversation (20 minutes). Jesus' statement about being the way, the truth and the life points out that faith in him is the key to salvation. Present this truth while remaining sensitive to the seekers in the group. You don't want to downplay the truth, but don't allow anyone to be overly dogmatic. Don't hammer seekers over the head with the exclusivity of Christ. Remember also that this is not just about life in eternity but life in the here and now.

Someone may ask how Jesus can claim to be the only way to God. Though there is not time to address this at length now, encourage the questioner to consider the claims of Jesus, his lifestyle and his actions. Does he act in harmony with God? Does he represent the heart and love of God? Avoid arguing about who is right and who is wrong. Simply ask the person to keep observing Jesus and keep asking questions. You can always point him or her to other resources that provide extended discussions of Jesus and his claims to be God in the flesh.

Connecting Our Stories (20 minutes). These questions may elicit stories about literally getting lost or feeling lost spiritually or emotionally. Either type of answer is fine. Often to find our way we must rely on someone or something to guide us—a person who gives us directions or a map. Sometimes we stumble upon something we recognize, and that helps point the way. If people tell a story of being physically lost, try to draw the analogy between a physical journey and our spiritual journey.

Trust issues are big in our culture. More than 50 percent of marriages end in divorce, so many people have grown up in a home where trust was broken. Add to that a general mistrust of authority, employers, government and the clergy, and you understand why skepticism prevails. Asking someone to trust Jesus implies that he is trustworthy. Emphasize *why* Jesus is trustworthy. His actions toward the poor, his concern for the marginalized, his inclusion of women, his keeping of promises and speaking the truth, his desire to honor the Father and not build an empire for himself, his humility, his sacrificial life, his respect for authority—all these point to someone who can be trusted.

Finding Our Way (10 minutes). Some may read Jesus' statement as saying that he is the only way to a relationship with the God of heaven, which believers know to be true. However, challenge group members to see that Jesus is also offering them a way to live right now, a life that is focused on the mission of sharing the love of God with others. The journey to our destiny does not start when we die; it begins now. Abundant life is available now. Salvation is not just what we get when we trust Jesus with our life. It is much more: salvation is a way of life. So we can say, as believers, that we have been saved (we have eternal life), we are being saved (as Jesus works in us now through the Holy Spirit) and we will be saved (ultimately from eternal separation from God).

It is important to emphasize the ongoing experience—sanctification—by which we become more like Jesus and grow in faith. Seekers need to see that Jesus is not simply a fire insurance policy to keep us from going to hell. He offers a full and rewarding life—now and forever.

Praying Together (about 10 minutes). Stress the invitation that Jesus is offering to all of us. Even if group members have accepted Christ as Savior and Forgiver, Jesus' words challenge them to ask themselves if they are actually living in the way and the life that Jesus modeled and calls us to.

For some seekers in your group, the next step may be trusting Christ with their life. Be aware of this possibility, and be prepared to help those who are ready to take this step.

SESSION 6.
JESUS CLARIFIES OUR CALLING.
Luke 5:1-11

Gathering to Listen (5 minutes). Listening to your life is not about self-absorption. It is about paying attention to the gifts and strengths and even the weaknesses that make up who you are. There are two dimensions to God's calling in our life. The first is that we are called to follow Jesus, to accept him as our forgiver and allow him to be our Lord, the One who takes control of our life—our destiny and our calling. We're called to be disciples—students—of Christ. We also have a second, more specific calling: a mission, task or vocation that God has designed for us, based on how we are gifted and wired. It is in relationship with Jesus that both of these aspects of calling are clarified.

Be prepared to hear some frustration among participants. Many people do not feel that their work expresses their gifts and experience. The job they hold and the vocation they desire are not the same—and the situation may not look like it will change any time soon. This is why it is very important to understand that we are called to become followers of Jesus, *whatever* our work might be. And we are all to be engaged in the work of Christ through a local church with others who share the call. We are not called to be alone.

If our work can be an expression of our deep passions and gifts, that's wonderful. But if not, we can still fulfill the calling given to every follower. Remember that 25 percent of people in Jesus' time and culture were slaves or indentured servants. They probably were not able to express much of their passion or gifts in their work, but they could be faithful and seek to fulfill God's call nonetheless.

Encountering Jesus (15 minutes). Jesus seems to be testing Simon while also building a friendship with him. The *New Bible Commentary* says, "Although Simon, as an experienced fisherman, knew that there was little likelihood of a catch, he was already sufficiently impressed by Jesus to obey his command." Jesus wanted Simon to feel the exhilaration of catching lots of fish, so that he could compare that to catching men and women for Christ, a much greater thrill.

Simon is skeptical but willing to give it a try. You almost wonder if under his breath he was muttering about rabbis not being experts in fishing, his area of skill. His response might have included a bit of sarcasm, or he might be making a simple gesture to honor a naive rabbi, or an act of honor and respect to an emerging Jewish leader. For the committed follower of Jesus, in any case, "because you say so" should be our mantra. Perhaps, like Simon Peter, we do not always remember with whom we are speaking.

Joining the Conversation (20 minutes). Callings come in the context of relationship. Participants may recall saying prayers like "If you are there, God . . ." very similar to Simon's "Because you say so, Master."

It is important to note that in Jesus' culture, rabbis were highly respected. The ultimate career for a young Jewish man was to enlist in a rabbinic school and become a rabbi (teacher). All their education from childhood through early adulthood was centered on learning the Jewish Scriptures and laws. At a certain point a boy might be deemed worthy of further study in the law. To do so required him to become a rabbi's apprentice. Boys in their teens would study hard and try to find rabbis who would accept them as an apprentice.

Simon Peter and his partners had likely never made the grade as boys. While little Joshua headed for schooling in the law, they had headed to the shores to work in their fathers' fishing business. They would never qualify as apprentices. They had a respectable but far from glamorous career. Then this special rabbi, Jesus, enters their lives. He teaches, heals the sick and performs many miracles. And to their surprise, he invites them to follow him, to become his apprentices. This was unusual: rabbis typically considered requests from potential apprentices but did not seek them out. Jesus' invitation was an honor beyond their wildest dreams. It makes perfect sense that they would follow him, even though they may have felt unworthy.

Simon understood that Jesus was even greater than a rabbi, that somehow he was a prophet or the Messiah. He felt ashamed and unworthy to be in Jesus' presence, but Jesus looked past that into his heart. And Jesus loved what he saw there.

Connecting Our Stories (20 minutes). Simon, Andrew, James and John were astonished at the great catch of fish. This fish story would surely be told all along the shores of Galilee for months to come.

This will not be the last time Jesus uses fish in teaching Simon Peter. In Matthew 17 he pulls two coins from the mouth of a fish to pay the temple tax for the two of them. And in John 21, to restore Peter after he had denied knowing him three times, Jesus again created a miraculous catch of fish.

Jesus' command, "Don't be afraid," is the most repeated command in the Bible. Although Simon would have been honored to be chosen by Jesus, he may have felt fear of being inadequate. Likewise, we often feel uncertain about following Jesus, wondering whether we are capable of hearing and following his call.

In the final question of this section, tapping into the fear of group members may be awkward. If your group is new, this may come slowly. You will have to lead the way and show an appropriate level of self-disclosure. Tell a bit about your own fears and struggles with becoming a "because you say so" follower of Jesus. But also realize that fear is a great motivator and can open people up to the work of God.

Finding Our Way (10 minutes). A lot of confusion surrounds the topic of callings. I have heard people say things like "The call to be a pastor is the highest calling God gives to mankind." That may encourage seminary students, but it is grossly unbiblical and unwarranted. The highest calling anyone can have is the one God gives them. Jesus called Matthew, a tax collector, to be part of his inner circle of apprentices. He became a great writer (just read the book of Matthew). And Jesus sent another tax collector, Zacchaeus, right back into the marketplace (Luke 19:1-10), because that was his calling.

Most callings are neither spectacular nor dramatic. Think rather in terms of conviction—doing something that is right and that you know God wants you to do. Encourage members to follow the leading of the Holy Spirit. Encourage seekers by assuring them that following Christ means finding greater clarity about who you are and what you are called to do and be in this life. It is a great adventure!

That being said, Jesus reminds us all that his followers are in the people-catching business. Regardless of where we work, we should all be involved in introducing people to the transforming love and power of Jesus.

We may not be called to leave our job and family to follow Christ—but we are called to put him first. Urge group members to wrestle with what that means. For some, it may mean something as radical as a job change. For others, it may mean simply an attitude adjustment. Be respectful of each person's right to move at their own pace. Avoid taking over God's job of clarifying someone else's calling; don't tell people what you think they ought to do. Ask questions and let them discover it themselves.

Praying Together (about 10 minutes). You may want to have group members pair up and pray for each other during the week. Again, the idea is not to fix or give advice but to help each other hear God more clearly.

Also available from InterVarsity Press and Willow Creek Resources

BIBLE 101. *Where truth meets life.*
Bill Donahue, series editor

The Bible 101 series is designed for those who want to know how to study God's Word, understand it clearly and apply it to their lives in a way that produces personal transformation. Geared especially for groups, the series can also profitably be used for individual study. Each guide has five sessions that overview essential information and teach new study skills. The sixth session brings the skills together in a way that relates them to daily life.

FOUNDATIONS: *How We Got Our Bible*
Bill Donahue

TIMES & PLACES: *Picturing the Events of the Bible*
Michael Redding

COVER TO COVER: *Getting the Bible's Big Picture*
Gerry Mathisen

STUDY METHODS: *Experiencing the Power of God's Word*
Kathy Dice

INTERPRETATION: *Discovering the Bible for Yourself*
Judson Poling

PARABLES & PROPHECY: *Unlocking the Bible's Mysteries*
Bill Donahue

GREAT THEMES: *Understanding the Bible's Core Doctrines*
Michael Redding

PERSONAL DEVOTION: *Taking God's Word to Heart*
Kathy Dice